Beyond the Mask

Uncovering the Hidden Strengths of Autism

Dr. Miles J. Cooper

Disclaimer

The information provided in Beyond the Mask: Uncovering the Hidden Strengths of Autism is intended for educational and informational purposes only. It is not a substitute for professional medical, psychological, or therapeutic advice, diagnosis, or treatment. Readers are encouraged to seek guidance from qualified professionals for specific concerns related to autism or other health conditions.

While every effort has been made to ensure accuracy, the author and publisher make no representations or warranties regarding the content's completeness, reliability, or applicability to individual circumstances. The experiences and insights shared in this book are general and may not apply to every individual on the autism spectrum.

This book is designed to promote understanding, inclusion, and empowerment. Readers are encouraged to use the strategies and perspectives provided as tools for growth while respecting the diverse and unique experiences of autistic individuals.

Table of contents

Introduction

The Reason for this Book: Shifting the Narrative on Autism

Autism, frequently examined from the perspective of challenges and limits, is considerably more than a determination or a condition to be made due. It is a special approach to encountering the world, described by uncommon perspectives and capacities that frequently stay unnoticed. For a long time, discussions around autism have been established in stereotypes and misconceptions, focusing in on shortfalls as opposed to strengths. This book looks to move that account by commending the secret strengths of autism and reexamining how we perspective neurodiversity.

The motivation behind this book is to move past the superficial comprehension of autism and jump into the significant, frequently neglected abilities that individuals on the spectrum bring to the world. Whether you are a person with autism, a parent, a teacher, or essentially somebody looking to extend your comprehension, this book expects to motivate another perspective— one that values validness, celebrates diversity, and advances strengthening.

By unmasking these secret strengths, we can encourage a more comprehensive and steady environment where individuals with autism make due as well as flourish. This change in context can change individual relationships, schooling systems, work environments, and society in general.

Figuring out Autism: From Challenges to Strengths

Autism is much of the time portrayed as a spectrum since it incorporates many capacities, strengths, and experiences. However, a large part of the discussion will in general fixate on what individuals with autism can't do, as opposed to their best. While challenges like tangible sensitivity, communication contrasts, or social troubles might exist, they are just a single piece of the story.

The other part — an account of inconceivable strengths — frequently stays untold. These strengths incorporate unrivaled tender loving care, uncommon memory, inventiveness, and creative critical thinking. They likewise incorporate emotional profundity, genuineness, and a capacity to move toward circumstances with a new point of perspective. By focusing in on these attributes, we can reexamine autism not as a shortage to be fixed, but rather as a special and significant approach to being.

This book challenges the regular story by investigating these secret strengths. It urges users to see past stereotypes and think about the full spectrum of human potential. Figuring out autism from this perspective benefits individuals on the spectrum and enhances society by embracing the worth of different personalities and experiences.

Why Recognizing Hidden Strengths Matters

The act of recognizing hidden strengths isn't simply a practice in positive thinking — it is a fundamental stage toward strengthening. Numerous individuals with autism face a world that anticipates congruity and frequently excuses their special strengths as whimsies or weaknesses. This cultural assumption can prompt masking, where individuals smother their real selves to fit in. While masking might give brief acceptance, it frequently comes at a massive expense to psychological well-being, confidence, and in general prosperity.

At the point when we recognize and support hidden strengths, we make a pathway for validness. By focusing on what compels individuals to be special and important, we can assist them to embrace their personality with certainty. This acceptance cultivates a feeling of having a place, decreases the strain to cover, and permits individuals to contribute their gifts in significant ways.

Past the individual effect, celebrating hidden strengths has extensive ramifications for families, communities, and society. Guardians can all the more likely help their kids by understanding their actual potential. Teachers can fit educational strategies to feature capacities instead of immediate apparent deficiencies. Bosses can take advantage of a wellspring of innovation by making comprehensive work environments.

The far-reaching influence of this quality-based approach can change cultural attitudes, testing inclinations and misinterpretations that have persevered for a really long time. It makes the way for a future where neurodiversity is praised as a resource, as opposed to seen as a responsibility.

The Journey Ahead

All through this book, we will investigate autism through another focal point — one that goes past challenges to reveal hidden strengths. Every part is intended to give understanding, procedures, and motivation to enable individuals with autism and the individuals who support them.

In the initial segment, we will dig into a more emotional comprehension of autism, moving past stereotypes to feature the one of a kind capacities and perspective it offers. We will likewise address the peculiarity of masking, investigating its effect and offering pathways to genuineness.

In the subsequent part, we will reveal the secret strengths of autism, focusing in on cognitive, emotional, social, and functional capacities that frequently stay disregarded. These strengths are significant for self-sensitivity as well as can possibly advance families, working environments, and communities.

At last, the book will give noteworthy systems to strengthen — assisting individuals with autism find and embrace their assets, fabricate steady conditions, and flourish in their credibility. From educational settings to proficient spaces, the strategies offered expect to encourage inclusivity, awareness, and a strengths based way to deal with neurodiversity.

Embracing Another Point of perspective

"Beyond the Mask" welcomes you to leave on an extraordinary journey — and journey of understanding, acceptance, and festivity. By revealing the secret strengths of autism, we can draw nearer to an existence where neurodiversity individuals are seen, esteemed, and enabled

This isn't simply a book about autism; it is a source of inspiration. It provokes us to reexamine our presumptions, separate obstructions, and embrace another story — one that praises the full spectrum of human potential.

The opportunity has arrived to look past the veil and find the remarkable strengths that lie underneath. Allow this book to act as an aide and a motivation as we push toward a fate of more prominent figuring out, consideration, and festivity of autism in the entirety of its aspects.

Part 1: Understanding Autism Beyond the Surface

CHAPTER 1: REDEFINING AUTISM

Moving Beyond Stereotypes

Autism has for quite some time been characterized by society through a restricted focal point, molded by stereotypes and obsolete discernments. These stereotypes frequently portray autism as a progression of shortages: a failure to mingle, an absence of compassion, or a repugnance for change. While certain attributes related to autism might introduce challenges, this distorted perspective neglects to catch the intricacy and lavishness of the autistic insight.

To genuinely comprehend autism, we should move past these superficial suspicions and embrace its diversity. Autism, or Autism Spectrum Disorder (ASD), is certainly not a solid condition but a spectrum of experiences, capacities, and strengths. No two autistic individuals are indistinguishable, similarly as no two neurotypical individuals are indistinguishable. Every individual's process is molded by a novel mix of strengths, strengths, and challenges, impacted by their current circumstance, childhood, and character.

Stereotypes distort autism as well as breaking point valuable opportunities for those on the spectrum. For instance, the legend that autistic individuals can't shape significant relationships might prompt social rejection, while the conviction that they can't succeed expertly may keep them from getting to satisfying vocations. These confusions make obstructions that ruin the capability of individuals with autism and add to shame.

Moving past stereotypes requires a change in outlook. It includes paying attention to the voices of autistic individuals, recognizing their lived experiences, and recognizing their commitments to society. By testing assumptions, we can make the way for a more comprehensive and exact comprehension of autism — one that celebrates diversity instead of underestimates it.

The Spectrum of Capacities and Experiences

The expression "spectrum" is integral to figuring out autism, yet it is frequently misjudged. Autism is definitely not a direct spectrum with "gentle" toward one side and "extreme" on the other. All things being equal, it is all the more precisely depicted as a multi-layered spectrum, including many capacities, strengths, and requirements. An individual might succeed in one region, like scientific reasoning, while at the same time confronting challenges in another, like tangible handling.

This changeability highlights the significance of surveying every individual as an individual, instead of sorting them in light of a one-size-fits-all determination. For instance, a few autistic individuals might have extraordinary verbal abilities and appreciate participating in emotional discussions, while others might impart nonverbally and utilize elective techniques, like composition or innovation, to put themselves out there.

The spectrum of autism likewise reaches out to past capacities to incorporate tangible experiences and emotional reactions. Numerous autistic individuals experience uplifted aversion to sounds, lights, or surfaces. While this can be testing, it additionally offers interesting perspective points and experiences into the environment that others might ignore.

Recognizing the full spectrum of autism destroys the possibility that it is exclusively a state of shortage. It features the diversity inside the autistic local area and advises us that strengths and challenges frequently exist together. This understanding is basic for encouraging acceptance and establishing conditions that help individual requirements and capacities.

Recognizing the Unique perspective of Autism

Autistic individuals frequently carry a new and significant point of perspective to the world. Their novel perspectives and seeing can prompt experiences and advancements that probably won't emerge from traditional strategies. For instance, individuals on the spectrum are frequently lauded for their capacity to consider some fresh possibilities, focus strongly around areas of interest, and move toward issues with a thorough outlook.

One of the most striking parts of autism is the capacity to see examples and organizations that others could miss. This expertise is especially apparent in fields like arithmetic, science, and innovation, where accuracy and logical reasoning are exceptionally esteemed. Be that as it may, it isn't restricted to specialized spaces. Autistic individuals have additionally made critical commitments to artistic expression, where their inventiveness and creativity sparkle.

The autistic point of perspective reaches out past scholarly and innovative pursuits. It likewise incorporates emotional profundity and credibility. While social organizations may here and there be testing, autistic individuals frequently structure emotional, veritable organizations with those they trust. Their genuineness, faithfulness, and commitment to relationships are characteristics that improve both individual and expert bonds.

By recognizing and esteeming these perspectives, we can start to see autism as a wellspring of solidarity and innovation instead of exclusively as a condition to be made due. This change in context benefits autistic individuals as well as enhances society overall, encouraging a diversity of thoughts and experiences.

Rethinking Autism for a Superior Future

Rethinking autism isn't tied in with disregarding its challenges however about surveying them in a setting with its assets. It is tied in with moving the concentration based on what is "off-base" to what is novel and important. This redefinition expects us to challenge predispositions, question suppositions, and teach ourselves about the real essence of autism.

A quality-based way to deal with autism can make groundbreaking impacts. For individuals on the spectrum, it cultivates self-acceptance and certainty, engaging them to embrace their personality unafraid of judgment. For families, it gives a structure to praising accomplishments and supporting innovation. For society, it advances consideration, understanding, and the acceptance of neurodiversity as a resource.

This section establishes the groundwork for a more emotional investigation of autism's secret assets, making way for a journey of revelation and strengthening. By moving past stereotypes, recognizing the spectrum of capacities, and esteeming the special point of perspective of autism, we can reclassify being autistic — and, in doing as such, make an additional comprehensive and merciful world.

CHAPTER 2: THE MASKING PHENOMENON

What Is Masking, and Why Does It Happen?

Masking, frequently alluded to as "disguising," is a survival technique utilized by numerous autistic individuals to explore social circumstances and measure up to cultural assumptions. It includes intentionally or unwittingly stifling ways of behaving and strengths related to autism while mirroring neurotypical standards. For example, somebody could drive themselves to keep in touch, smother stimming (self-mitigating innovations), or practice social content to show up more socially capable.

Masking emerges as a reaction to outside pressures, especially in conditions where being "unique" is met with judgment, rejection, or misconception. From early on, autistic individuals might get unobtrusive or obvious messages that their regular ways of behaving are unsatisfactory. These messages could emerge out of friends, teachers, relatives, or the media, supporting that fitting in requires masking their actual selves.

For some, masking turns into a method for surviving — a method for staying away from derision, tormenting, or prohibition. In expert or scholarly settings, masking can act to get opportunities or stay away from segregation. In any case, this survival strategy frequently comes at a massive expense. The work expected to keep up with the façade can be genuinely and sincerely debilitating, prompting burnout, tension, and a feeling of detachment from one's bona fide self.

While masking might give momentary benefits, it eventually features a cultural inability to establish comprehensive conditions where neurodiversity is recognized and esteemed. Understanding masking is an urgent move toward encouraging acceptance and enabling individuals to act naturally unafraid of judgment or dismissal.

THE Effect of Masking on Emotional and Psychological well-being

The emotional and cognitive cost of masking is significant. Continually smothering one's regular propensities and taking on ways of behaving that vibe unnatural can prompt constant pressure and tension. This emotional strain frequently appears as insecurities or an inescapable apprehension about being "found out."

One of the main outcomes of masking is burnout. In contrast to ordinary fatigue, autistic burnout is a condition of outrageous physical, cognitive, and emotional exhaustion brought about by delayed masking and overstimulation. Burnout can weaken day-to-day working, decrease capacity to bear tangible information, and intensify co-happening conditions like discouragement and tension.

Masking can likewise dissolve a singular's feeling of character. After some time, the line between valid ways of behaving and the covered persona can become obscure, making it hard for the individual to reconnect with their actual self. This disengagement can prompt sensations of forlornness and confinement, even in friendly circumstances where the individual has all the earmarks of flourishing.

Besides, the cultural assumption to veil builds up destructive stereotypes about autism. At the point when autistic individuals cover themselves effectively, it can sustain the legend that they needn't bother with help or that their challenges are unimportant. This confusion can bring about an absence of facilities and understanding, further intensifying the hardships faced by those on the spectrum.

Recognizing the inconvenient impacts of masking highlights, the requirement for more noteworthy awareness and acceptance. By encouraging conditions where autistic individuals have a real sense of security to put themselves out there truly, we can relieve the pessimistic effects of masking and advance cognitive and emotional prosperity.

Unmasking: Steps Towards Authenticity

Unmasking is the method involved with reclaiming one's bona fide self and embracing characteristics and ways of behaving that were recently covered up. This journey is emotionally private and frequently requires critical cognitive fortitude, as it includes testing cultural assumptions and defying emotionally imbued fears of judgment or dismissal.

The most vital phase in unmasking is awareness. This includes recognizing the ways of behaving and techniques used to veil and figuring out the explanations for them. For some, this interaction is worked with by associating with the autistic local area, where shared experiences can give approval and advocacy. Gaining from other individuals who have explored the journey of unmasking can be both engaging and rousing.

Making places of refuge is basic for unmasking. Places of refuge — whether at home, school, or work — are conditions where individuals feel acknowledged and esteemed for what their identity is. In these spaces, autistic individuals can investigate their personalities unafraid of analysis or avoidance. Relatives, companions, teachers, and bosses assume a fundamental part in encouraging these conditions by showing acceptance, understanding, and regard.

One more significant part of unmasking is self-promotion. This includes conveying one's requirements and inclinations to other individuals, for example, mentioning tangible facilities or making sense of one of a kind communication styles. While self-advocacy can be testing, it is an amazing asset for building relationships in perspective of shared regard and understanding.

Restorative help can likewise support the unmasking system. Working with experts who comprehend autism can assist individuals with exploring the emotional intricacies of shedding the cover. Treatment can give systems to overseeing uneasiness, building self-assurance, and embracing one's personality.

At last, cultural change is fundamental for supporting exposure. This incorporates advancing awareness and acceptance of autism, testing stereotypes, and supporting approaches that oblige neurodiversity needs. At the point when society values genuineness and diversity, individuals feel engaged to act naturally without the requirement for masking.

The Way Toward Acceptance

The peculiarity of masking features the strain among distinction and cultural assumptions. It mirrors a world that frequently focuses on congruity over legitimacy, leaving numerous autistic individuals feeling concealed and underestimated. Nonetheless, change is conceivable.

By understanding what masking is and why it works out, we can start to destroy the frameworks and perspectives that sustain it. Making a culture of acceptance includes something other than enduring contrasts — it requires praising them and recognizing the exceptional strengths and points of perspective that autism brings to our communities.

For autistic individuals, the journey of unmasking isn't tied in with leaving the abilities they've grown, however, about reclaiming the opportunity to act naturally. It's tied in with tracking down balance: knowing when to adjust and when to embrace credibility. For society, the journey includes making spaces where this equilibrium can be accomplished, permitting everybody to flourish.

As we push ahead, let us recollect that authenticity isn't simply a gift we give ourselves; it's a gift we provide for the world. By supporting unmasking and cultivating acceptance, we make a more extravagant, more comprehensive society where each individual can sparkle past the cover.

CHAPTER 3: REFRAMING CHALLENGES AS STRENGTHS

The Role of Neurodiversity in A Changing World

The idea of neurodiversity praises the regular varieties in human brains and recognizes that distinctions in cognitive working are not shortages but rather fundamental parts of the human diversity. Autism is one of the many types of neurodiversity, and understanding its worth is crucial in a quickly developing world. As innovation progresses and cultural standards shift, there is a developing requirement for extraordinary perspectives and creative critical thinking draws near — strengths frequently intrinsic in autistic individuals.

Neurodiversity challenges customary ideas of what is thought of as "typical" or "utilitarian." It underscores that all types of reasoning and handling enjoy their benefits, particularly when applied to perplexing and diverse challenges. For instance, autistic individuals frequently show uplifted focus, design acceptance, and creativity, characteristics that are essential in fields like innovation, science, workmanship, and social advancement.

The impacting scene progressively esteems inclusivity, versatility, and creativity — characteristics that line up with the strengths of neurodivergent individuals. Organizations are starting to recognize that assorted groups drive advancement, and many are embracing comprehensive recruiting practices to take advantage of the interesting strengths of neurodiversity workers. By reexamining autism not as a bunch of challenges but rather as a wellspring of potential, society can open an unimaginable wellspring of ability and creativity.

How Seen Impediments Can Become Extraordinary Resources

Challenges related to autism, like tangible responsive strengths or hardships with social connection, are many times misjudged as outlandish boundaries. In any case, these apparent limits can be reexamined as novel resources, particularly when seen from the perspective of individual strengths and inclinations.

Sensory Sensitivities as a Benefit

While sensory sensitivities can present challenges in overwhelming conditions, they additionally consider elevated discernment and scrupulousness. This intense sensory awareness can be especially important in fields that require accuracy, like workmanship, plan, culinary expressions, and quality control. For instance, an autistic person with uplifted hear-able responsiveness could succeed in music synthesis or sound designing, while somebody with a sharp visual sense could flourish in visual communication or photography.

Direct Communication Styles

Social corporations can now and then be trying for autistic individuals, especially when deciphering unwritten social standards. In any case, numerous autistic individuals speak with unequivocal quality and genuineness, attributes that can encourage clearness and confidence in private and expert relationships. In conditions that esteem straightforwardness, for example, project the board or information examination, this communication style can be a critical strength.

Focused Interests Prompting Skill

Autistic individuals frequently foster extreme, focused interests, at times alluded to as "exceptional interests." While these interests might be misjudged as fanatical, they habitually lead to emotional skill and imaginative reasoning. For example, somebody enthusiastic about cosmology could contribute weighty bits of knowledge to the field, while one more individual emotionally keen on coding could succeed as a product engineer.

Transformation as a Flexibility Expertise

Exploring a world that frequently doesn't oblige autism requires huge versatility. This capacity to change and persist notwithstanding challenges encourages flexibility, a quality that is important in both individual and expert lives. Versatility empowers individuals to handle challenges, gain from experiences, and keep endeavoring toward their objectives.

The Significance of a Strengths Based Approach

A strengths based approach moves the concentration from how an individual can't treat what they can accomplish. This point of perspective enables autistic individuals as well as challenges cultural stereotypes that frequently limit opportunities.

In Education

Conventional schooling systems frequently focus on congruity and normalized strategies, which might ignore or underestimate the strengths of autistic understudies. By embracing a strengths-based approach, teachers can fit learning conditions to individual necessities, underscoring gifts and interests. For example, an understudy with uncommon numerical capacities could profit from cutting-edge coursework in that subject, regardless of whether they battle in different regions like language expressions.

In the Working environment

Consolidating a strengths-based approach in the working environment includes making roles and undertakings that line up with a singular's capacities and inclinations. For instance, somebody with an ability for design acceptance could succeed in information examination, while one more person with solid hierarchical abilities could flourish in managerial roles. Bosses who embrace this outlook cultivate a more comprehensive environment as well as get to the undiscovered potential that can drive innovation and efficiency.

In Self-sensitivity

For autistic individuals, a strengths-based approach supports awareness and self-acceptance. Remembering one's own assets can build certainty and give an establishment to chase after significant objectives. This perspective likewise advances a feeling of organization, permitting individuals to advocate for their necessities and inclinations.

Embracing the Capability of Neurodiversity

Rethinking challenges as strengths require a change in outlook, both at an individual and cultural level. For autistic individuals, it includes embracing their special capacities and recognizing that their disparities are significant commitments to the world. For society, it requests a pledge to inclusivity and a readiness to challenge assumptions about autism.

This shift starts with schooling and awareness. By finding out about the different experiences and capacities of autistic individuals, we can move past stereotypes and value the profundity of their commitments. Public awareness crusades, comprehensive strategies, and representation in media assume a vital part in molding a seriously tolerating and understanding society.

Moreover, partners — whether they are relatives, teachers, bosses, or companions — can have a tremendous effect by taking on a quality-based outlook. Supporting autistic individuals in distinguishing and sustaining their assets benefits them as well as improves the communities and organizations they are important to.

A Future Focused on Strengths

Reevaluating challenges as strengths isn't tied in with disregarding the hardships that accompany autism; rather, it is tied in with recognizing that these challenges exist together with mind-blowing potential. By taking on a strengths-based approach, we can make a reality where autistic individuals are esteemed for what their identity is and upheld in accomplishing their fullest potential.

In embracing neurodiversity, society moves toward a future that commends distinction and encourages innovation. The exceptional strengths of autistic individuals are not only resources to be utilized — they are tokens of the extravagance and intricacy of the human experience. At the point when we focus around strengths, we enable individuals as well as build a more comprehensive and even-handed world for all.

Part 2: Uncovering and Nurturing Hidden Strengths

CHAPTER 4: COGNITIVE STRENGTHS

Exceptional Memory and Attention to Detail

Perhaps of the most surprising cognitive strength numerous autistic individuals display is uncommon memory. This strength can appear in changed structures, like eidetic memory (recalling pictures with striking subtlety) or long-term maintenance of realities, figures, and experiences. Autistic individuals frequently have an exceptional capacity to recollect and precisely recall explicit information, whether it relates to individual occasions, scholarly subjects, or expert errands.

This outstanding memory isn't restricted to repetition remembrance. It frequently reaches out to examples, cycles, and organizations, considering top to bottom getting it and critical thinking. For instance, an autistic individual could recall perplexing subtleties from a discussion quite a while back, empowering them to give significant settings in private or expert settings.

Meticulousness supplements this memory strength. Autistic individuals are frequently exceptionally perceptive, seeing subtleties and nuances that others could neglect. This capacity is important in roles requiring accuracy and exactness, like exploration, information examination, quality confirmation, or imaginative undertakings like altering or planning.

Saddling these strengths in educational and proficient conditions includes setting out opportunities for autistic individuals to apply their itemized focus. Whether it's creating particular learning projects or planning work roles that accentuate their assets, these transformations can open their maximum capacity.

Critical thinking and Insightful Reasoning

Autistic individuals frequently approach critical thinking and logical undertakings with a particular point of perspective. As opposed to following customary strategies, they might succeed in distinguishing alternative solutions, breaking new ground, and enhancing in manners that challenge laid-out standards. This strength emerges from their capacity to think emotionally, consider factors completely, and process information in novel ways.

For instance, in technology and engineering fields, autistic experts have added to progressions by distinguishing failures, enhancing cycles, and creating effective fixes. Also, in scholarly community and examination, their scientific reasoning permits them to investigate new speculations and challenge suppositions, driving advancement in different disciplines.

This fitness for critical thinking is likewise clear in regular day-to-day existence. From coordinating a family task proficiently to investigating complex frameworks, autistic individuals carry a deliberate and careful way of dealing with challenges. By recognizing and sustaining this strength, families, teachers, and managers can engage autistic individuals to succeed in roles that require imaginative reasoning.

Harnessing Creativity and Innovation

Creativity and innovation are trademark attributes among numerous autistic individuals. In opposition to stereotypes that outline autism exclusively as far as rationale and unbending nature, numerous autistic individuals have an exceptional limit concerning creative ideas and imaginative articulation. This innovativeness frequently comes from their capacity to see the world through a one-of-a-kind focal point, unhampered by traditional assumptions or suppositions.

In human expression, autistic individuals have made wonderful commitments to music, painting, writing, and film. However, their innovativeness isn't restricted to conventional imaginative fields. Many additionally succeed in regions like programming advancement, design, and enterprising endeavors, where imaginative reasoning is exceptionally esteemed.

One clarification for this innovative strength is how autistic brains process information. By focusing in emotionally on subjects of interest and framing flighty organizations, autistic individuals can produce original thoughts and approaches. For example, somebody energetic about natural supportability could foster an imaginative reusing framework, while one more with an interest in narrating could create convincing stories that challenge cultural standards.

To sustain inventiveness and innovation, critical to give conditions energize investigation and self-articulation. Whether through craftsmanship programs, innovation studios, or mentorship opportunities, cultivating spaces where autistic individuals can trial and offer their thoughts is fundamental.

Recognizing the Worth of Cognitive Strengths

The cognitive strengths of autistic individuals are significant not exclusively to them but additionally to the more extensive society. Uncommon memory, tender loving care, critical thinking abilities, and creativity are characteristics that advance communities, drive innovation, and move progress. In any case, recognizing and supporting these strengths requires a change in the way we perspective and oblige autism.

Instead of focusing in exclusively on shortages or challenges, teachers, bosses, and partners should take on a strengths-based approach. This perspective accentuates what autistic individuals can accomplish and features the potential for their commitments to reshape ventures, impact culture, and work on regular daily existence.

Supporting Cognitive Strengths in Practice

To completely outfit cognitive strengths, it's fundamental to make frameworks that help autistic individuals find and apply their capacities. Here are a few procedures for encouraging these strengths:

Education: Customized learning plans that emphasis areas of interest can assist autistic understudies with succeeding scholastically. For example, integrating their assets into subjects like math, science, or craftsmanship can support certainty and accomplishment.

Work environment Consideration: Managers can plan roles and undertakings that line up with a person's cognitive assets. Giving facilities, like calm work areas or adaptable hours, can additionally upgrade efficiency and fulfillment.

Local area Projects: Neighborhood drives, like studios or clubs, can urge autistic individuals to investigate their inclinations and foster their abilities in strong conditions.

Family and Social Help: Families and companions assume an essential part in recognizing and celebrating cognitive strengths. Empowering investigation, offering acclaim for accomplishments, and pushing for amazing opportunities are imperative advances.

THE Effect of Cognitive Strengths

At the point when upheld and recognized, the cognitive strengths of autistic individuals can have broad effects. These strengths contribute not exclusively to individual satisfaction yet additionally to progressions in innovation, workmanship, science, and that's only the tip of the iceberg. By esteeming and putting resources into these capacities, we move toward building an additional comprehensive and inventive world.

Cognitive strengths are not simply benefits for autistic individuals — they are resources for society overall. Through schooling, awareness, and advocacy, we can open this potential and commend the diversity that makes humankind flourish.

CHAPTER 5: EMOTIONAL AND SOCIAL STRENGTHS

Empathy in Unexpected Forms

One of the most misunderstood parts of autism is compassion. Traditional accounts frequently depict autistic individuals as lacking sympathy, yet this is a long way from reality. Numerous autistic individuals experience compassion in significant and novel ways, frequently associating emotionally with feelings that others might ignore.

Autistic sympathy can appear as an intense aversion to the sensations of others. For example, somebody on the autism spectrum could feel an extreme emotional reaction while seeing foul play, bitterness, or delight in someone else. This elevated awareness now and again brings about overpowering feelings, making it trying for them to communicate sympathy in socially anticipated ways. Notwithstanding, their interior experience of compassion is certifiable and emotionally felt.

This sensitivity frequently reaches out to past human organizations which include creatures, nature, or even unique ideas. For instance, an autistic individual could advocate enthusiastically for basic entitlements or natural protection, driven by areas of strength for an association with these causes.

Recognizing this type of compassion requires looking past customary articulations, like verbal consolation or noticeable emotional responses. By getting it and valuing the profundity of autistic compassion, society can move past misguided judgments and cultivate more comprehensive relationships.

Loyalty and Trustworthiness in Relationships

Autistic individuals are much of the time described by an unfaltering feeling of reliability. At the point when they structure organizations — whether with companions, family, or partners — they will quite often put emotionally in keeping up with and respecting those relationships. Their devotion frequently originates from their worth driven way to deal with corporations, where trust and responsibility hold critical importance.

This dedication can appear as predictable help, steadfastness, and a readiness to remain by others through challenges. Autistic individuals frequently focus on legitimacy in their relationships, esteeming higher expectations without compromise with regard to kinships and organizations.

Trustworthiness is one more sign of numerous autistic individuals' social organizations. They frequently impart straightforwardly, without the channels or social misrepresentation that can convolute collaborations. While this straightforwardness could some of the time be confounded as gruffness, it mirrors a reviving straightforwardness that many individual's perspectives as dependable and solid.

In this present reality where credibility is progressively esteemed, the genuineness and unwaveringly of autistic individuals act as a wakeup call of the significance of significant organizations. Their relationships, however once in a while less in number, are many times wealthy in trust and common regard.

Extraordinary Communication Styles
Communication styles among autistic individuals are as different as the autism spectrum itself. Some might favor verbal articulation, while others succeed in nonverbal or composed communication. Understanding and adjusting to these extraordinary styles can open further organizations and encourage shared understanding.

For a few autistic individuals, verbal communication could include exact, strict language. This can be a strength in conditions where clearness is fundamental, like specialized fields or scholarly settings. Their capacity to verbalize considerations with accuracy frequently takes out vagueness and improves joint effort.

Nonverbal communication is another region where autistic individuals frequently succeed. They might utilize signals, looks, or imaginative mediums, for example, workmanship or music to communicate their feelings and thoughts. For instance, an autistic craftsman could catch complex feelings through visual narrating, offering experiences that rise above words.

Written communication is a specific strength for the overwhelming majority autistic individuals. The chance to handle contemplations and pass them on through composing considers rich, nuanced articulation. In web-based communities, online journals, and expert settings, autistic individuals much of the time contribute remarkable points of perspective that enhance conversations and flash innovation.

To help these one of a kind communication styles, fundamental to establish conditions are versatile and comprehensive. Empowering elective types of articulation, giving chances to composed or visual communication, and rehearsing persistence in discussions are successful ways of improving comprehension and association.

Recognizing the Worth of Emotional and Social Strengths

Emotional and social strengths among autistic individuals challenge cultural standards and stereotypes about how individuals ought to communicate. These strengths, while at times capricious, add to the wealth of human diversity and give significant examples in sympathy, devotion, and validness.

By recognizing and esteeming these strengths, society can make a culture of incorporation that celebrates instead of underestimates the one of a kind commitments of autistic individuals. Emotional and social strengths, when recognized and sustained, enhance individual relationships, proficient conditions, and communities.

Supporting Emotional and Social Strengths

Supporting these strengths requires a methodology grounded in compassion, regard, and adaptability. Here are a few procedures to consider:

Building Trust: Laying out protected and steady conditions assists autistic individuals with feeling open to communicating their feelings and building relationships. Trust is the establishment for opening emotional and social strengths.

Empowering Self-Articulation: Giving opportunities to imaginative outlets, like craftsmanship, composing, or music, permits autistic individuals to share their feelings and points of perspective in manners that vibe normal to them.

Esteeming Authenticity: Underlining the significance of genuineness and devotion in relationships commends the strengths autistic individuals bring to their communications.

Advancing Comprehensive Communication: Adjusting specialized strategies to suit individual inclinations — whether verbal, nonverbal, or composed — cultivates further organization and shared understanding.

The Effect of Emotional and Social Strengths

At the point when recognized and upheld, the emotional and social strengths of autistic individuals extraordinarily affect families, work environments, and communities. These strengths rouse a more emotional appreciation for different approaches to interfacing and add to a more comprehensive society.

Autistic individuals teach us that sympathy, steadfastness, and trustworthiness are not limited by cultural assumptions. All things being equal, they show the way that emotional and social strengths can take many structures, each offering exceptional worth and experiences. By embracing these strengths, we make a world that values credibility, celebrates diversity, and flourishes with significant organizations.

CHAPTER 6: PRACTICAL STRENGTHS FOR EVERYDAY LIFE

Building Skills in Routine and Organization

Perhaps the most remarkable useful strength numerous autistic individuals have is their capacity to lay out and keep up with schedules. While schedules are many times seen as a strategy for dealing with stress for overseeing vulnerability, they likewise address a huge strength in association and productivity. Autistic individuals much of the time succeed at organizing their day-to-day routines in manners that boost efficiency and limit pressure.

For example, a few autistic individuals make definite timetables to deal with their time successfully, guaranteeing that errands are finished with accuracy and consistency. This capacity to separate complex cycles into reasonable advances isn't just gainful in private life yet in addition exceptionally esteemed in expert and scholastic settings.

Also, their inclination for request and consistency can add to their amazing hierarchical abilities. From carefully organizing things in their current circumstance to creating frameworks that upgrade the work process, autistic individuals frequently carry clearness and build to turbulent circumstances.

To harness this strength, families, teachers, and businesses can empower the advancement of hierarchical instruments like organizers, agendas, or digital applications. Recognizing and commending these abilities helps build certainty and shows the way that daily practice and association can be a wellspring of strengthening.

Adjusting to Change and Creating Strength

While autistic individuals are frequently connected with an inclination for schedule, they likewise show impressive strength while adjusting to change — particularly when upheld such that regards their necessities. Adjusting to change isn't just about overseeing inconvenience but about creating strategies to explore new conditions, relationships, and challenges.

Resilience is apparent in the manner numerous autistic individuals approach critical thinking. When confronted with startling changes, they frequently track down inventive ways of changing and keep up with security. This strength can be especially important in unique or high speed conditions where adaptability is fundamental.

The capacity to foster flexibility is as often as possible established in the emotionally supportive communities around them. Families, teachers, and bosses who give clear communication, slow advances, and understanding can assist autistic individuals with adjusting with certainty. Over the long run, these experiences fabricate a healthy identity viability and encourage the capacity to confront new circumstances with fortitude and assurance.

Focusing on Long-term Objectives

Autistic individuals frequently display a noteworthy capacity to focus in seriously on areas of interest or significance. This focus can convert into a strong strength for laying out and accomplishing long-term objectives. Whether seeking after energy, succeeding in a vocation, or adding to a reason, their commitment and determination are key drivers of progress.

This strength is particularly apparent in fields that require supported effort and tender loving care. For instance, an autistic person with a strong fascination with coding could commit a long time to dominating programming dialects and creating inventive programming. Essentially, somebody energetic about civil rights could focus on long-term promotion work, utilizing their concentration and assurance to drive significant change.

Accomplishing long-term objectives frequently includes defeating snags, which features another practical strength: determination. Autistic individuals much of the time show a capacity to manage challenges sincerely, even despite misfortunes or errors.

To help this strength, it's critical to give opportunities to objective setting and celebrate achievements. Consolation and affirmation of progress can build up their responsibility and build trust in their capacities.

Recognizing the Worthy of Useful Strengths

Useful strengths like daily practice, association, versatility, and focus are many times neglected in conversations about autism. However, these strengths are fundamental for exploring daily existence and making progress in different spaces. By recognizing and supporting these capacities, society can engage autistic individuals to flourish in their own and proficient lives.

These down-to-earth strengths benefit autistic individuals as well as add to their families, working environments, and communities. From making requests in complex circumstances to driving long-term projects forward, their capacities enhance the existence of everyone around them.

Supporting Practical Strengths

To completely saddle useful strengths, fundamental to establish conditions to support and praise these capacities. Here are a few strategies:

Empowering Schedules: Giving apparatuses like organizers, schedules, and authoritative applications can help autistic individuals create and keep up with powerful schedules.

Working with Advances: Clear communication and slow changes can facilitate the most common way of adjusting to change, encouraging strength and certainty.

Advancing Objective Setting: Empowering individuals to set reasonable, significant objectives and offering help in accomplishing them can build confidence and inspiration.

Observing Accomplishments: Recognizing achievements, regardless of how little, builds up the worth of down-to-earth strengths and energizes further innovation.

The Effect of Practical Strengths

Practical strengths assume a fundamental part in emotionally shaping the existences of autistic individuals, assisting them with exploring challenges, accomplish objectives, and contribute definitively to their communities. These strengths, when recognized and upheld, become integral assets for individual and expert achievement.

By embracing these capacities, society moves toward cultivating incorporation and understanding. Commonsense strengths are not only resources for autistic individuals — they are significant commitments to the world, offering illustrations in perseverance, association, and versatility.

The down to earth strengths of autistic individuals help us to remember the extraordinary potential inside diversity. By supporting these strengths, we set out opportunities for innovation, association, and shared achievement, fabricating a more comprehensive and engaged society.

Part 3: Strategies for Empowerment

CHAPTER 7: SUPPORTING SELF-DISCOVERY

Creating Safe Spaces for Authentic Expression

For autistic individuals, the journey to self-disclosure frequently starts with the foundation of conditions where they have a real sense of reassurance to communicate their actual selves. Places of refuge are actual areas as well as emotional and social conditions liberated from judgment, strain to adjust, or unreasonable assumptions.

In these spaces, autistic individuals can investigate their contemplations, sentiments, and interests unafraid of misconception or dismissal. This opportunity cultivates authenticity, empowering them to embrace their novel characteristics and reveal hidden strengths. Steady conditions frequently incorporate clear communication, regard for sensory inclinations, and affirmation of individual necessities.

Guardians, teachers, and partners assume a basic part in making these places of refuge. For example, study halls can be adjusted with tangible agreeable facilities, working environments can execute calm zones, and families can lay out schedules that regard individual inclinations. By focusing on inclusivity, these conditions energize self-articulation and awareness.

Empowering Individual Interests and Passions

Autistic individuals frequently exhibit extreme concentration and energy for explicit areas of interest. These interests, sometimes referred to as "unique interests," are not simply leisure activities; they are strong roads for self-revelation and self-sensitivity. Drawing in with these interests can prompt a more emotional comprehension of one's capacities, desires, and potential.

At the point when individual interests are supported, they frequently advance into remarkable strengths that can be applied in different settings. For instance, an interest with innovation could prompt a lifelong in programming improvement, while an adoration for creatures could motivate work in veterinary sciences or creature support. Empowering these interests assists autistic individuals with associating with their real selves and fabricating trust in their capacities.

Families and coaches can uphold these interests by giving assets, like books, classes, or devices, and by praising accomplishments around there. Also, setting out opportunities for social collaboration around shared interests can cultivate significant organizations and diminish sensations of separation.

Observing Individual Accomplishments

Self-disclosure is a course of recognizing and commending one's achievements, regardless of how little. For autistic individuals, each move toward understanding their assets and capacities is an achievement worth recognizing. These accomplishments could incorporate dominating another expertise, conquering an individual test, or just inclination happier with communicating their thoughts.

Acknowledgement and festivity are fundamental since they approve the singular's endeavors and energize further investigation of their true capacity. This doesn't mean setting unreasonable assumptions or compelling them to perform; all things being equal, it includes regarding progress such that feels significant and engaging.

Commending accomplishments can take many structures. It could include imparting their victories to friends and family, making a portfolio of their work, or essentially considering their journey in an individual diary. These practices support confidence as well as assist autistic individuals with building a positive cognitive self-portrait.

The Role of Help in Self-Disclosure

Self-revelation is seldom a singular journey. For autistic individuals, the help of understanding and humane partners is important. Guardians, teachers, friends, and experts can give direction, support, and assets that assist individuals with investigating their character and potential.

Advocacy can appear as mentorship, where believed individuals share bits of knowledge and experiences, or promotion, where partners work to eliminate obstructions and set out opportunities. It likewise incorporates consistent encouragement, like tuning in without judgment and offering consolation during snapshots of uncertainty or trouble.

By cultivating a culture of acceptance and support, partners can assist autistic individuals with exploring the intricacies of self-revelation with certainty and lucidity.

Empowering Self-Disclosure Through Assets
Assess to assets is a vital part of self-disclosure. These could incorporate books, online communities, support gatherings, or treatment benefits that give apparatuses and bits of knowledge to self-improvement. For instance, autistic individuals could profit from treatment meetings focused in on building awareness or studios that show new abilities lined up with their inclinations.

Innovation likewise assumes a critical part in supporting self-disclosure. Applications and stages intended for neurodiversity individuals can assist with communication, association, and investigating individual interests. Virtual entertainment and online discussions can give spaces to association and self-articulation, empowering individuals to share their experiences and gain from others.

The Effect of Self-Disclosure
The process of self-revelation is extraordinary. For autistic individuals, it includes moving past cultural assumptions and stereotypes to embrace their remarkable character and strengths. This journey upgrades their personal satisfaction as well as empowers them to contribute genuinely to their communities and the world overall.

Self-disclosure cultivates flexibility, certainty, and a feeling of direction. It enables individuals to advocate for themselves, put forth objectives that line up with their strengths, and fabricate relationships that regard their authenticity. In addition, it challenges the cultural perspective of autism, featuring the strengths and commitments of neurodiverse individuals.

Supporting Self-Disclosure as a group

The journey of self-disclosure is emotionally private, however it is additionally formed by the collective endeavors of families, communities, and society. By making inclusive spaces, empowering exploration, and praising uniqueness, we can uphold autistic individuals in revealing their actual potential.

In doing as such, we engage them to flourish as well as improve how we might interpret diversity and human potential. Supporting self-revelation is a common obligation that benefits everybody, cultivating a reality where credibility and uniqueness are commended.

Through self-discovery, autistic individuals get comfortable with themselves, their assets, and their spot on the planet. By supporting this journey, we move toward building a more comprehensive, understanding, and engaging society.

CHAPTER 8: BUILDING A STRENGTHS-BASED FRAMEWORK

Identifying Strengths in Educational and Work Environments

In educational and work settings, conventional strategies frequently focus around challenges and shortages, particularly for autistic individuals. However, a strengths-based structure shifts the perspective to feature and expand upon innate capacities and gifts. This approach enables autistic individuals and upgrades the general environment by cultivating consideration and expanding potential.

In schools, distinguishing strengths starts with customized learning. Autistic understudies, like science, imaginative expressions, or innovation, frequently succeed in unambiguous regions. Teachers can notice these abilities through understudy execution, interests, and ways of behaving, fitting guidance to exploit them. For instance, an understudy with an excellent memory could profit from exercises including point-by-point investigation or verifiable examinations.

Additionally, working environments can uphold autistic representatives by recognizing their one-of-a-kind commitments, like uplifted concentration, accuracy, and critical thinking abilities. Bosses can carry out strengths-based appraisals during enrollment and execution assessments, guaranteeing roles line up with individual abilities and giving clear directions, organized assignments, and facilities, such as adaptable timetables or tangible amicable work areas, further upgrading efficiency and occupation fulfillment.

By taking on a quality-focused approach, teaching, and workplaces become more comprehensive, steady, and equipped for encouraging accomplishment for all individuals.

Utilizing Technology and Tools for Progress

Innovation is a strong partner in supporting autistic individuals to understand their assets and accomplish their objectives. From assistive devices to inventive stages, innovation can upgrade communication, learning, and expert innovation.

For instance, applications intended to work on hierarchical abilities, like errand the board or planning instruments, can assist individuals with using time effectively and focus. Discourse to-message applications empower more straightforward communication for the individuals who find verbal articulation testing. Likewise, web based mastering stages give opportunities to expertise improvement in a controlled, adaptable environment that suits individual inclinations.

In work environments, advances like cooperative apparatuses, versatile programming, and virtual conditions permit autistic representatives to work productively while obliging their necessities. For example, surrounding sound blocking earphones can moderate sensory sensitivity, while video conferencing empowers remote work choices.

Guardians, teachers, and managers can team up to distinguish and coordinate the right devices, guaranteeing availability and usefulness. By utilizing innovation actually, autistic individuals can beat obstructions and upgrade their assets in different settings.

Developing Self-Advocacy Skills
Self-advocacy is a foundation of a strengths based system. It enables autistic individuals to communicate their requirements, state their freedoms, and take responsibility for strengths and objectives. Fostering these abilities requires a mix of teaching, practice, and advocacy.

Showing self-advocacy starts with encouraging awareness. Autistic individuals need potential chances to investigate their capacities, figure out their challenges, and eloquent their inclinations. This can include directed conversations, intelligent activities, or mentorship from other individuals who share comparable experiences.

In educational settings, educators can energize self-advocacy by including understudies in laying out private objectives or taking part in individualized education plan (IEP) gatherings. In work environments, training projects can help representatives to really discuss with bosses and associates, empowering them to address concerns and propose solutions unhesitatingly.

Encouraging groups of individuals, including families, companions, and experts, likewise assume an essential part in building self-promotion abilities. Consolation, approval, and direction can ingrain certainty and inspiration, assisting autistic individuals with exploring complex social and expert conditions.

The Significance of a Strengths Based Mindset

A strengths based system isn't simply a bunch of practices; an outlook values diversity, celebrates uniqueness, and trusts in the capability of each and every individual. This perspective challenges stereotypes about autism, stressing the extraordinary commitments autistic individuals bring to society.

At the point when communities embrace a strengths based mindset, they encourage a culture of acceptance and consideration. This social shift benefits autistic individuals as well as society on the loose by opening creative thoughts, different points of perspective, and undiscovered gifts. Schools and working environments that embrace this mindset frequently see further developed confidence, expanded cooperation, and better progress in all cases.

Executing the Structure in Day-to-day existence

A strengths based system ought to stretch out past proper conditions into day-to-day existence. Families can take on this methodology by empowering side interests, commending accomplishments, and giving opportunities to self-sensitivity. For instance, a parent who sees their kid's interest with examples could acquaint them with coding or configuration, sustaining both their advantage and potential profession valuable opportunities.

In companionships and social interactions, focusing in on strengths advances shared regard and understanding. Featuring the interesting characteristics of autistic individuals can develop relationships, fortify communities, and move more extensive acceptance of neurodiversity.

Working for the Future

The strengths based system establishes the groundwork for a more promising time to come, where autistic individuals can flourish as their genuine selves. By recognizing, supporting, and commending strengths, this approach engages individuals as well as changes communities.

This structure empowers a cooperative effort among teachers, businesses, families, and society to establish conditions that recognize and esteem the commitments of each and every person. It is a pathway toward more prominent consideration, innovation, and understanding, opening the enormous potential inside the neurodiverse populace.

By building a strengths based system, we move toward a world that esteems each individual's exceptional assets and capacities, making ready for a more comprehensive and enabling society.

CHAPTER 9: STRENGTHS IN COMMUNITY AND SOCIETY

Breaking Barriers Through Sensitivity and Inclusion

Communities blossom with diversity, yet confusion about autism frequently creates hindrances that limit the incorporation of autistic individuals. Breaking these boundaries begins with bringing issues to light and encouraging comprehension. Awareness isn't just about understanding what autism is; it's tied in with recognizing the strengths, gifts, and commitments of autistic individuals.

Educational campaigns, media representation, and grassroots drives assume imperative parts in moving cultural discernments. Featuring examples of overcoming adversity of autistic individuals in different fields — whether in innovation, workmanship, or local area administration — provokes stereotypes and moves others to see past the mark. These accounts represent that autism isn't a constraint however an extraordinary point of perspective that can enhance society.

Incorporation goes past awareness. It requires significant stages to establish conditions where autistic individuals feel esteemed and upheld. Public spaces can take on sensory well-disposed plans, while occasions can offer facilities like calm zones and open specialized devices. Schools and working environments ought to give preparation to staff to be all the more likely to comprehend and uphold neurodiverse individuals. By focusing on incorporation, communities encourage having a place and open the capability of every part.

Building Significant Connections

At the core of a strengths-based way to deal with autism lies the significance of relationships. Building significant organizations requires effort from both autistic individuals and their communities. Autistic individuals frequently have extraordinary communication styles, which can prompt misconceptions. Be that as it may, with persistence and a readiness to learn, relationships can prosper.

Friendships and family relationships are fortified when individuals focus around common regard and understanding. For example, as opposed to anticipating that an autistic individual should adjust to conventional accepted practices, loved ones can adjust their communication to suit individual inclinations. This could include giving additional opportunity for reactions, being expressed in discussions, or regarding sensory limits.

Mentorship programs additionally give significant opportunities to associations. Autistic individuals can profit from the direction presented by coaches who comprehend their experiences, assisting them with exploring challenges and investigating opportunities. Then again, tutors and friends gain bits of knowledge from different points of perspective, cultivating sympathy and coordinated effort.

Local area organizations can additionally uphold organizations through clubs, meetups, and interest-based bunches custom-fitted for neurodiverse individuals. These spaces energize valid articulation, make shared experiences, and fortify the texture of the local area.

The Role OF Partners in Supporting Autism

Partners assume a basic part in making a more comprehensive society. A partner is somebody who effectively supports and promotes autistic individuals, guaranteeing their voices are heard and their assets recognized. Partners can be companions, relatives, teachers, associates, or local area pioneers.

The initial step to being a partner is education. Understanding the extraordinary experiences and strengths of autistic individuals' outfits aligns with the information to challenge inclinations and supporters. Partners can utilize this information to address destructive stereotypes, advance exact representations of autism, and impact strategy changes that benefit neurodiverse communities.

Listening is similarly fundamental. Partners ought to focus on paying attention to autistic individuals, esteeming their feedback and regarding their independence. This includes setting out opportunities for autistic individuals to share their perspectives and inclinations in discussions, dynamic cycles, and support endeavors.

Advocacy is one more key part of allyship. Partners can enhance autistic voices by supporting drives that advance consideration, for example, working environment diversity programs or administrative changes. They can likewise go about as middle individuals in circumstances where autistic individuals face segregation or need admittance to chances.

Eventually, being a partner implies being an accomplice in making a world that commends contrasts and embraces neurodiversity. It requires responsibility, empathy, and activity to guarantee autistic individuals flourish inside their communities.

The Effect of a Strengths-Based Individual Group

At the point when communities focus on strengths as opposed to shortages, the effect stretches out a long way past individuals. A quality-based local area is one where each part is esteemed for their one-of-a-kind commitment. This outlook encourages innovation, joint effort, and flexibility.

For instance, a school that embraces a strengths-based approach might see further developed understudy commitment, as neurodiverse students feel engaged to share their gifts. Additionally, working environments that focus on incorporation frequently experience expanded innovativeness and critical thinking, as different perspectives add to dynamic solution.

Strengths-based communities additionally rouse cultural change. As acceptance develops, boundaries decrease, making ready for policies and practices that advance value and availability. From available foundations to comprehensive widespread innovations, these progressions benefit everybody, not simply autistic individuals.

Making a Cultural Acceptance

Acceptance goes past resilience; it includes embracing contrasts as important and fundamental. Making a culture of acceptance requires progressing effort from individuals, organizations, and society at large.

Schooling is vital to developing acceptance. Schools and work environments can incorporate illustrations on neurodiversity into their educational plans and training programs, empowering compassion and understanding. Public campaigns can feature the accomplishments and perspectives of autistic individuals, normalizing their presence in all everyday issues.

Representation matters too. At the point when autistic individuals see themselves reflected in media, administrative roles, and local area roles, it supports their worth and potential. Representation additionally challenges stereotypes, showing the world the broadness of abilities and experiences inside the autism spectrum.

Local area pioneers, policymakers, and organizations should likewise focus on openness and value. By putting resources into assets that help autistic individuals —, for example, professional preparation programs, sensory agreeable offices, and socially encouraging groups of individuals — communities exhibit their obligation to consideration.

The Fate of Neurodiversity in the Society

As awareness develops, so does the potential for a general public that values neurodiversity. What's in store lies in a coordinated effort, where communities, organizations, and establishments cooperate to guarantee autistic individuals can contribute completely and truly.

This vision requires collective work to destroy obstructions, enhance strengths, and celebrate contrasts. It challenges obsolete models of similarity and embraces the wealth of assorted points of perspective. By building strengths in the local area and society, we make an establishment for progress, innovation, and empathy — an existence where everybody can flourish.

Through these endeavors, society elevates autistic individuals as well as improves itself. The commitments of autistic individuals are important, and their incorporation prepares for a more brilliant, more comprehensive future. Together, we can assemble communities where strengths are praised, hindrances are broken, and potential outcomes are boundless.

Part 4: Thriving Beyond the Mask

CHAPTER 10: CREATING A FUTURE OF POSSIBILITIES

Real-Life Stories of Strength and Resilience

Autistic individuals have consistently shown that the human soul is equipped for striking accomplishments, even notwithstanding challenges. Their accounts enlighten the force of diligence and the significance of embracing contrasts. For instance, Sanctuary Grandin, an autistic promoter and teacher of creature science, changed the agrarian business by upsetting compassionate animals taking care of practices. Her capacity to think outwardly and her assurance to channel her special perspective into inventive solutions have enlivened millions.

Also, Anthony Ianni, the principal autistic Division I school ball player, has shared his journey of beating difficulty to accomplish his fantasies. His promotion work accentuates the significance of self-conviction and local area support in setting out opportunities for progress. These accounts exhibit that versatility, when joined with acceptance of strengths, can prepare for exceptional achievements.

Genuine models feature a basic truth: each autistic individual can contribute definitively to society whenever offered the chance. By focusing on strengths and cultivating comprehensive conditions, society can open secret potential and make a universe of conceivable outcomes.

Recognizing the Worth of Neurodiverse Points of Perspective

Diversity is a foundation of innovation, and neurodiversity offers points of perspective that challenge customary reasoning. Autistic individuals frequently succeed in fields requiring accuracy, creativity, and critical thinking. Their meticulousness, obligation to exactness, and capacity to break new ground have added to headways in science, innovation, and human expression.

For example, numerous tech organizations have executed neurodiversity recruiting drives, recognizing that autistic workers have unmatched abilities in role programming, data analysis, and online protection. By esteeming these extraordinary gifts, organizations gain an upper hand while cultivating a more comprehensive labor force.

Past expert settings, and neurodiverse perspectives improve communities and relationships. Autistic individuals frequently approach issues with new bits of knowledge, offering solutions that could somehow be disregarded. Their commitments advise us that innovation flourishes when different perspectives are commended.

Recognizing and esteeming neurodiverse perspectives isn't simply an ethical objective; it is a pathway to building more grounded, more unique communities. By embracing these strengths, society can separate stereotypes and prepare for individuals in the future to flourish.

Tracking down Purpose and Satisfaction

Reason and satisfaction are widespread desires, and autistic individuals are no exception. Making an eventual fate of conceivable outcomes includes assisting autistic individuals with finding their interests and giving the devices and advocacy expected to seek after them.

For the overwhelming majority of autistic individuals, design is established to their greatest advantage. Whether it's dominating a particular point, succeeding in an imaginative undertaking, or adding to a reason they care about, these interests act as an establishment for significant lives. Empowering investigation and commending accomplishments, regardless of how little, can motivate certainty and drive.

Relatives, teachers, and local area pioneers assume a critical part in directing autistic individuals toward reason. This could include recognizing opportunities that line up with their assets, interfacing them with tutors, or encouraging conditions where their abilities can thrive. For instance, somebody with a strong fascination with mechanics could flourish in an apprenticeship program, while a person with extraordinary creative abilities could track down satisfaction in displaying their work at neighborhood shows.

Reason additionally rises out of legitimate organizations. Kinships, mentorships, and joint efforts assist autistic individuals with building communities that help self-improvement and shared objectives. These organizations underline the significance of common comprehension and regard, making pathways for satisfaction that stretch out past individual achievement.

Engaging Autistic Individuals to Dream Big

An eventual fate of potential outcomes starts with strengthening. Empowering autistic individuals to think beyond practical boundaries and giving them the assets to accomplish those fantasies is significant. Strengthening isn't just about eliminating boundaries; it's tied in with outfitting individuals with the abilities, certainty, and valuable chances to characterize their prospects.

Self-advocacy is a foundation of strengthening. Showing autistic individuals how to convey their necessities, put down stopping points, and explore challenges encourages freedom and fearlessness. It likewise guarantees they have a voice in choices that influence their lives. For instance, self-support abilities can assist somebody with arranging facilities in the work environment or expressing their inclinations in private relationships.

Education and training are additionally basic. Schools, professional projects, and local area organizations should focus on strengths based on getting the hang of, fitting opportunities to individual capacities and interests. Innovation can assume an extraordinary part, offering instruments and stages that help expertise improvement and openness.

Strengthening stretches out to testing cultural standards and assumptions. Empowering autistic individuals to seek unusual ways or resist stereotypes motivates others to reconsider their suspicions about autism. At the point when society upholds enormous dreams, the potential outcomes become boundless.

Encouraging a Collective Vision for the Future

Making an eventual fate of conceivable outcomes isn't the obligation of autistic individuals alone; it requires collective effort. Families, teachers, businesses, policymakers, and communities all play a part in molding a comprehensive world.

Families can establish conditions where autistic individuals feel esteemed and upheld. By praising accomplishments and giving unrestricted consolation, families ingrain certainty and versatility. Also, teachers can adjust their teaching methods to support abilities, offering customized guidance that assists understudies with arriving at their maximum capacity.

Managers have a unique opportunity to tackle the strengths of autistic individuals by executing neurodiversity drives. Adaptable recruiting rehearses, mentorship programs, and comprehensive workplaces empower autistic representatives to flourish. These endeavors benefit individuals as well as drive advancement and creativity inside organizations.

Policymakers can support consideration by upholding regulation that upholds openness, education, and opportunities for autistic individuals. Putting resources into local area assets, for example, sensory amicable offices and particular help programs guarantees that nobody is abandoned.

Communities should cooperate to cultivate acceptance and understanding. Public campaigns, encouraging groups of individuals, and social drives can separate obstructions and advance a common vision of consideration. At the point when society focuses on this vision, what's in store becomes more splendid for everybody.

Observing the Journey Ahead

The journey toward a fate of conceivable outcomes is continuous, and each forward-moving step merits celebrating. As society keeps on embracing neurodiversity, the way becomes more clear for autistic individuals to accomplish their fantasies and contribute definitively to the world.

This section fills in as an update that what's to come isn't fixed; it is formed by our collective activities and attitudes. By focusing on strengths, encouraging consideration, and engaging individuals to arrive at their true capacity, we can make a reality where each autistic individual has a valuable chance to flourish.

What's to come is loaded with conceivable outcomes — conceivable outcomes that honor the interesting perspectives and gifts of autistic individuals while improving society all in all. Together, we can build a future that celebrates diversity, champions consideration, and rouses significance.

CHAPTER 11: ADVOCATING FOR CHANGE

Challenging Misconceptions About Autism

Misinterpretations about autism remain one of the main boundaries to understanding and acceptance. Many stereotypes depict autism as a condition exclusively characterized by shortfalls or challenges, ignoring the diversity and strengths inside the autistic local area. Testing these confusions is basic to cultivating a more comprehensive and informed society.

One of the most unavoidable fantasies is that autistic individuals need compassion. While they might communicate feelings in an unexpected way, numerous autistic individuals have significant sympathy and care emotionally about others. Reexamining these distinctions as varieties in communication as opposed to shortages cultivates more noteworthy comprehension.

Another normal misguided judgment is that autism is a one-size-fits-all conclusion. The fact of the matter is undeniably more mind-boggling: autism exists on a spectrum, incorporating many capacities, challenges, and perspectives. Recognizing this diversity permits us to see the value in the remarkable commitments of every individual as opposed to keeping them to a restricted generalization.

Media representation likewise assumes an essential part in molding public discernment. Autistic characters in motion pictures or Television programs are in many cases portrayed in misrepresented or unreasonable ways, which can support destructive stereotypes. Supporting legitimate representation, informed by input from the autistic local area, can assist with destroying these obsolete thoughts.

Educational efforts are fundamental for fighting misinterpretations. Studios, courses, and public campaigns can give exact information about autism, assisting with supplanting fantasies with a more emotional appreciation for neurodiversity. By encouraging comprehension and compassion, these endeavors make an establishment for significant change.

Cultivating Inclusivity in Schools, Working Environments, and Communities

Inclusivity starts with establishing conditions where autistic individuals feel esteemed, regarded, and upheld. This requires fundamental changes in schools, work environments, and communities to guarantee that everybody has the chance to flourish.

In Schools, inclusivity begins with early mediation and individualized help. Teachers and heads can embrace strength-based approaches, focusing on what understudies can do as opposed to what they can't. Training teachers to recognize and sustain the remarkable gifts of autistic understudies creates a culture of acceptance and support. Adaptable showing strategies, sensory agreeable study halls, and companion mentorship projects can additionally improve inclusivity.

Work environments are one more basic region for cultivating inclusivity. Organizations that embrace neurodiversity benefit from the uncommon abilities autistic representatives frequently offer of real value, for example, tender loving care, innovative critical thinking, and dependability. Executing facilities like adaptable work hours, tangible cordial spaces, and clear communication practices can engage autistic representatives to succeed. Organizations like Microsoft and SAP have driven the way with neurodiversity recruiting drives, demonstrating that inclusivity isn't just moral but also great for business.

Communities assume an essential part in making comprehensive spaces where autistic individuals can interface, develop, and flourish. Public venues, libraries, and sporting offices can offer sensory well-disposed projects and exercises intended to oblige assorted needs. Public campaigns and occasions, like Autism Awareness Month, can advance comprehension and acceptance at a more extensive level.

Inclusivity is not a one-time effort but a continuous responsibility. By effectively looking for input from autistic individuals and their families, schools, work environments, and communities can ceaselessly improve and adjust to address their issues.

Inspiring a Shift Towards a Strengths-Based Mindset

A strengths based outlook moves the concentration from deficiencies to capacities, enabling autistic individuals to embrace their special gifts and commitments. This point of perspective underscores possible impediments, to testing the conventional clinical model of autism that frequently focuses on finding and mediation over strengthening.

Advancing a strengths-based outlook begins with language. The words we use to portray autism matter. Rather than outlining autism as a problem to be "fixed," we can depict it as an alternate approach to encountering the world. This unobtrusive yet strong change in language impacts how autistic individuals see themselves and how others see them.

In schooling, a strengths-based approach includes distinguishing and supporting the special gifts of every understudy. For instance, an understudy with serious areas of strength for memory could succeed in workmanship or planning, while one more enthusiastically for numbers could flourish in math or information examination. Fitting education to individual strengths supports certainty as well as makes way for future achievement.

In the work environment, a strengths-based mindset urges businesses to see past customary recruiting standards and recognize the worth of neurodiverse points of perspective. By matching roles to a singular's capacities, organizations can take advantage of extraordinary abilities that drive innovation and efficiency.

Guardians and parental figures likewise assume a pivotal part in taking on a strengths-based mindset. Celebrating little triumphs, empowering investigation, and giving opportunities for innovation assist autistic individuals with fostering a positive cognitive self-portrait and a feeling of organization.

Society overall benefits from this change in context. At the point when we focus on what autistic individuals can do, as opposed to what they can't, we open an abundance of undiscovered possibilities. This approach engages individuals as well as advances communities and drives progress.

The Power of Advocacy and Allyship

Advocacy is a useful asset for making change. By intensifying the voices of autistic individuals and their families, supporters can impact approaches, challenge stereotypes, and advance consideration.

Autistic self-advocates are at the cutting edge of this innovation, sharing their experiences to teach others and push for fundamental change. Their accounts feature the significance of paying attention to autistic points of perspective and including them in dynamic cycles. Organizations like the Autistic Self Advocacy Network (ASAN) give stages to autistic individuals to lead the discussion about autism and neurodiversity.

Partners likewise assume an urgent part in advocacy endeavors. Partners — whether they are relatives, teachers, colleagues, or companions — can utilize their situations to challenge segregation, advance consideration, and back autistic individuals in accomplishing their objectives. Powerful allyship includes tuning in, learning, and making a move to make a fairer society.

Advocacy can take many structures, from grassroots campaigns to official endeavors. For instance, pushing for strategies that guarantee admittance to school, medical care, and business opportunities for autistic individuals can have a significant effect. Advocacy likewise includes testing cultural standards and it is praised for making spaces where diversity.

A Collective Way Ahead

Pushing for change isn't the obligation of one individual or gathering — it requires collective effort. Families, teachers, businesses, policymakers, and communities should cooperate to make a reality where autistic individuals can flourish.

This collective way ahead includes progressing education, open dialogue, and a pledge to consideration. By testing confusions, cultivating inclusivity, and embracing a strengths-based mindset, we can build a general public that strengthens and celebrates neurodiversity. Advocacy isn't just about further developing results for autistic individuals; it is tied in with making a superior, more sympathetic world for everybody.

As this part closes, it fills in as a source of inspiration for users to become advocates for change. Whether it's by testing stereotypes, supporting inclusive strategies, or paying attention to and esteeming the experiences of autistic individuals, each work adds to a more promising time to come. Together, we can rouse a shift toward figuring out, acknowledging, and strengthening — opening the capability of autism beyond the mask.

Conclusion

Autism isn't a restriction but a spectrum of special strengths ready to be recognized and celebrated. Beyond the Mask: Uncovering the Hidden Strengths of Autism welcomes users to move their perspective, moving past stereotypes to embrace the diversity of experiences inside the autistic local area. By understanding the effect of masking, reevaluating challenges as strengths, and embracing a strengths-based outlook, we reveal the exceptional capability of autistic individuals.

Enabling autistic individuals begins with cultivating self-disclosure, building comprehensive conditions, and advocating their abilities in schools, working environments, and communities. Support is essential to destroying confusion and creating an even-handed world that values neurodiversity perspectives.

This journey isn't just about working on the existence of autistic individuals — it's tied in with enhancing society in general. We open ways to innovation, sympathy, and association by recognizing and supporting these secret strengths.

Allow this book to act as both an aide and a source of inspiration. Celebrate diversity, challenge obsolete standards, and focus on a future where everybody's one-of-a-kind commitments are esteemed. Together, we can make an existence where autism is recognized as the truth about a wellspring of solidarity and perpetual chance.